Prayer – Discover the Power Within

By Bonnie L. Bair

Life Improvements 2

Galesburg, Illinois

Names: Bair, Bonnie L.| Bair, Bonnie L. editor

Title: *Prayer – Discover the Power Within* | by Bonnie L. Bair

Description: 1st edition. | Galesburg; Illinois: Life Improvements 2, 2021

Identifiers: LCCN 2021904818 print

ISBN: 978-0-9994772-4-3

Independently published

Dedicated to Those Searching for God

Prayer – Discover the Power Within

5 Part Series on Prayer

Part 1   What is Prayer?

Part 2   Types of Prayer

Part 3   Prayer Interference

Part 4   Effective/Powerful Prayer

Part 5   Model Prayer

Part 1   What is Prayer?

Two-way intimate communication

Conversation with God

Intentional/purposeful

Occasional or constant (1)

Sincere

A drawing near to God

Direct addressing of God

Verbal or mental (1)

Sharing of feelings – pouring out the soul (1)

Asking in faith

Listening intently

Respectful

Honest – Trusting

Interested

Responsive to

Believing in each other

(1) Denotes Definitions from Webster's Dictionary

As humans, we like to be heard and understood, cooperated with, and loved. It feels good. It creates a feeling of specialness. God likes it too.

Conversely, we don't like inattention, being ignored, the silent treatment, being disregarded, or harsh tones from others. It feels bad. God doesn't like it either.

We all know what it's like to try to communicate with someone when there are distractions, interruptions, noise, etc. It doesn't work very well. It's frustrating!

We also don't enjoy interacting with someone who repeatedly hurts us, or blatantly ignores what we say. And we don't like it when someone talks to us only when they want something from us.

God probably feels the same way.

We may avoid the person and be silent or be non-cooperative with the other person - when this happens. God may too. We were created in God's image.

1st Peter 3:16 reads: the eyes of the Lord are on the righteous and His ears are attentive to their prayer. But the face of the Lord is against those who do evil.

It feels good when someone who has hurt us, genuinely apologizes and makes things better.

It feels good when someone pays attention to our needs and cooperates with us.

It feels good when someone listens.

It feels good when someone actively shows interest in us and talks to us and asks questions.

God likes this too!

It feels good when we trust the other person cares enough about who we are and what we need, that they will answer our questions and help us.

God likes this too!

Prayer is two-way communication.

When it feels like we are getting the silent treatment from God, it may be because of not listening intently, not asking questions with the expectation of an answer, being distracted, or ignoring God's word.

The pollution of sin makes two-way communication difficult.

In Isaiah 59:2, it says that sin builds barriers between us and God that causes God to hide His face from us, so He will not hear us.

1 Peter 3:16 reads: God's face is against those who do evil, but His eyes are on the righteous and His ears are attentive to their prayers.

Repenting clears the air and helps us to see, hear, smell, feel, and taste the presence of God.

1 John 1:19 says: If we confess our sins, God is faithful and just to forgive us our sins and to cleanse us from all unrighteousness.

When God is silent it may not always be because of sin. It may be because God is watching and waiting for us to move next, like in a chess game. Or God could just be enjoying watching us, knowing, and trusting us to do according to His will.

1 John 3:21 reads: If our hearts do not condemn us, we have confidence before God and receive from him anything we ask because we obey God's commands and do what pleases God.

Matthew 11:15 reads; he who has ears, let him hear.

God wants us to hear Him.

God is everywhere and God speaks to us in various ways at various times - through God's word, nature, our spouses and children, our Pastors, our friends, or even our enemies or TV.

A new thought may pop into our head after we ask a question. Or we might feel a gentle leading or pull in a certain direction. We might, at certain times, get a word directly from God to Us; a thought that doesn't seem like our own, a whisper to our soul, or an impression or word.

God also speaks to us and teaches us through situations and experiences.

In James 4:18 it says, as we draw close to God, God draws close to us. Various scriptures tell us that God inhabits the praise of his people.

(God likes being serenaded by those he loves and who love Him.) We like it too - like when others sing Happy Birthday to us.

God wants us to communicate with Him and God wants to answer us.

We need to attentively listen, trust and believe. Expect an answer.

Zechariah 13:9, "...they will call on my name and I will answer them; I will say, 'They are my people,' and they will say, 'The Lord is our God.'"

In Hebrews 4:16, we are told to come boldly to the throne of grace, that we may obtain mercy and find grace to help in time of need. In Hebrews 11:6 we

are told that God rewards those who seek Him.

In summary, **Prayer** is:

> **Two-way communication with God that is direct, sincere, respectful, honest, believing, and responsive.**

> **God speaks to us/answers us in various ways.**

> **Sin & distraction separate us from God.**

God Promises in 2 Chronicles 7:14

"If my people who are called by my name will humble themselves and pray and seek my face and turn from their wicked ways, then I will hear from heaven, and I will forgive their sin and heal their land."

Part 2   Types of Prayer

To review, prayer is a two-way intimate communication/relationship with God that includes God listening to Us and Us listening to God. It requires trust and honesty. Is respectful and responsive. It requires belief in each other.

When we establish a relationship with God by accepting Jesus as our Savior, and we ask the Holy Spirit of God to live in us, we become the temple of the Holy Spirit and God lives in us.

We like to be understood, cooperated with, and loved. God likes this too. Prayer is intentional and purposeful. It requires intent listening on both God's part and Our part - for a sincere and intimate relationship.

Types of Prayer/Communication with God

Praise/Adoration/Honor – Acknowledging God's greatness. Let all the upright in heart praise God. Example: *God you are most high above the earth. Your mercy and love are never-ending.*

Thanksgiving – Being thankful for something/one. Example: *Thank you for*

your goodness toward us. Thank you for your love and provision.

Petition/Supplication or Requests – Begging or Asking God for something or for help. Example: *Lord, I ask you to protect us on our trip and keep us safe.*

Intercessory Prayer – Asking God to help someone else. Example: *I pray for you to heal my friend and ask for you to help her and her family.*

Prayer of Confession/Repentance – Admitting to sin and asking for help to keep from sinning. Example: *Lord, I ask you to forgive me for being self-centered.*

Prayer of Agreement – Agreeing with what God's word says and that it is true. Example: *Lord, your word is true, and you love us. You tell us to come boldly to your throne and ask for help in time of need.*

Prayer of Acknowledgement/Understanding – Acknowledging God's nature/feelings/love. Example: *You are a good God. You know us so well and what we need. You must get frustrated when we don't do what your word says.*

Prayer (in Tongues) or Praying in the Spirit
(Speech or Song) – Allowing the Holy Spirit
within us to pray on our behalf, especially
when we don't know how or what to pray.
(1 Cor 14:15 & Romans 8:26). Build yourselves up
by praying in the Holy Spirit. (Jude 20).

Prayer of Authority – Asking God or agreeing
with God to take authority over the enemy.
Example: *In the name of Jesus Christ your
Son, we ask you to bind Satan in this situation
and render him useless. Lord, we ask you to
keep us from temptation/deliver us from evil.*

Part 3   Prayer Interference

What Can Interfere with our Prayers/Relationship with God, and what to do about it?

The 3 things that can disturb or interfere with our relationship with God are:

Sin/Satan/Distractions

What can we do to keep a close relationship and powerful prayer?

Honor God – Make God, and God's Word, a Priority.

> If we do not learn or remind ourselves of God's teaching by reading or hearing and studying God's word, we cannot keep God's teaching. God says, if anyone loves me, they will keep my teaching. Other things that consume our time/thinking over God (such as money, TV work, x-box, etc.) take away from our relationship with God and our prayer effectiveness and can become a form of idolatry. There should be no other God's before our God. (Exodus 20:2)

Pray with Right Motives – Have pure motives to follow God and God's word.

Be Thankful – In every situation by prayer and petition, with thanksgiving, present your requests to God. (Phil. 4:6)

Right Speech – Do not use God's name in vain. (Exodus 20:7) Speak the truth. Speak in line with God's word.

The Lord is against those who do evil. We are to keep our tongue from evil, refrain from guile, seek peace, and do right. Whoever loves life and desires to see many good days. Keep your tongue from evil and your lips from speaking lies. Turn from evil and do good; seek peace and pursue it (Psalm 34:12-14) God listens to those who pursue peace and whose lips are pure. The eyes of the Lord are upon the righteous and his ears are attentive to their prayers. (Psalm 34:15)

Right Living/Behavior – Behave as God's word says to behave. Living in ways that do not please God, hinders our prayers.

Living in ways that please God, helps our prayers be effective. His eyes are on the

righteous and he listens to their prayers (Psalm 34:15).

Confessing Sin – Repent/apologize for bad behavior/speech and unbelief. Unconfessed sin will hinder our prayers. It is sin that separates us from God. God is patient with us, not wanting anyone to perish, but everyone to come to repentance. (2 Peter 3:9)

Being Thankful – In every situation by prayer and petition, with thanksgiving, present your requests to God.

Forgiveness – Forgive yourself and others and maybe even God. Keep relationships honest. Not forgiving will hinder our prayers. Therefore, we must forgive others so that God will forgive us. If we have anything against anyone, we are to forgive them so that our Father in heaven will forgive our sins. We are not to return evil for evil but instead, give a blessing. (Romans 12:17-21)

Our relationships with others can affect our prayer life. We are to be sympathetic, brotherly, kindhearted, and humble. And to bless those that are unkind to us. (Matt 5:44)

Husband's, likewise, live with your wives in an understanding way, as with a weaker vessel, since she is a woman, and grant her honor as a fellow heir of the grace of life, so that your prayers are not hindered. (1 Peter 3:7) Wives, submit to your husbands in everything, so no one speaks badly about God. (Ephesians 5:22)

Honoring the Sabbath – Isaiah 58:13-14: If you keep your feet from breaking the Sabbath and from doing as you please on my Holy day if you call the Sabbath a delight and the Lord's holy day honorable, and if you honor it by not going your own way and not doing as you please or speaking idle words, then you will find your joy in the Lord and I will cause you to ride on the heights of the land and to feast on the inheritance of your father Jacob. The mouth of the LORD has spoken.

Resisting Satan – In James 4:7, we are told to submit ourselves to God and resist the devil and he shall flee from us.

Since the devil prowls around looking for who he can devour, we must be aware of his schemes and be vigilant at resisting.

3 examples of Resisting Satan

1. **Hermit's Knoll** – Satan flees at even a whisper of the name of JESUS. Once when by myself at night sleeping in the back of my car, 3-4 guys in a car (who had been drinking) came along and got out right next to my car (with bad intentions), saying, "What do we have here?" At which time I was frantically praying and asking the Lord "What should I do? What should I do?" The thought "Call out my name" came to me. Being so scared, I barely squeaked out a whisper of "Jesus". Within 2 seconds, the guys got in the car, the 3-4 doors slammed shut at the same time, and the car was gone!

   Praise Jesus when feeling low or attacked. Satan can't stand it and will leave.

2. **Hawaii** – While in Hawaii, my husband had heart issues. His heart had stopped many times and he was experiencing arrhythmias. While waiting to go to the operating room, I whispered "Satan, you cannot have my husband, you must leave him alone. In the name of Jesus Christ be gone!" In less than 10 seconds, Todd's heart converted back to sinus rhythm and he was saved from having to have two very risky procedures.

3. **Feeling attacked from all directions**, I said "Satan, you have to stay at least 50 feet away from myself and my family at all times from now on, in the name of Jesus Christ!" That same evening, I saw a small gray snake in the driveway. It was coiled and its head was up 5 inches in the air and was in a striking pose. It did not move. Our friend Mike saw it too. Mike kicked

the snake to see if it was alive. Although its head was up in a striking pose, it was deader than a doornail and was exactly 50 feet from our front door!

Put on the full armor of God – so, we can stand against the devil's schemes. (Ephes. 6:11)

The armor of God includes:

a) The helmet of salvation - Accepting Jesus Christ as our Lord and Savior protects our mind and being.

b) The breastplate of right living protects our hearts.

c) The belt of truth keeps our pants up and keeps us from becoming embarrassed.

d) When we shod our feet with the gospel of peace, we go to others in peace and are safer.

e) As we carry the <u>shield of faith</u> we go in confidence in God's word, which quenches the fiery darts of the enemy.

f) As we take up and use the <u>sword of the spirit</u>, (which is the *word of God*) – we kill the enemy. It reminds Yourself and Satan about what God's word says and the truth of God's word will help us to resist Satan and fight against him.

Ask God to keep us from temptation and evil. Jesus told us to pray this. It is included in the Lord's prayer.

Pray with gusto! – In James 5:16 we learn the effective intense prayer of a righteous person benefits much!

Part 4   Effective/Powerful Prayer

(Discover the Power Within)

If we have given our lives to God by accepting Jesus as our Savior, and asking the Holy Spirit to live in us, the Holy Spirit dwells within us and we become the temple of the Holy Spirit. Luke 11:13 reads: Jesus said: **If you are evil and know how to give good gifts to your children, how much more will your Father in heaven give the Holy Spirit to those who ask him!**

In Ephesians 6, we are told to be strong in the Lord and God's mighty power.

God's word instructs us to pray in the spirit on all occasions with all kinds of prayers and requests and to always keep on praying for all the Lord's people (Ephesians 6:18).

We are told to seek the Lord while he may be found and call on him while he is near. In Isaiah 55:6 and James 5:13 we are instructed: that if any of us are suffering, we should pray. And to come boldly to the throne of grace that we may obtain mercy and find grace to help in time of need (Hebrews 4:16).

The 7 PowerPoints of Powerful Prayer – Praise, Purity, Perseverance, Prayer (in the Spirit), Fasting, Praying in Pairs, Praying in the Name of Jesus.

1. **Praise makes prayer powerful.**

   Praise – Webster's dictionary defines praise as an expression of warm approval or admiration of, or to express one's respect and gratitude toward (especially in song).

   (Satan hates it when we praise God – It's like when we hear nails against a chalkboard.)

   We are told that God inhabits the praise of his people. In Psalm 96:1 We are encouraged to continually offer up a sacrifice of praise to God.

   Psalm 33:1 says: Praise is comely for the upright – meaning "suitable."

   Praise gives honor to God. Whosoever offers praise, glorifies me (Psalm 50:23).

2. **Purity makes prayer powerful.**

Purity – According to Webster's dictionary, purity is freedom from contamination – it's innocence.

Purity is doing our best to do as God wants. The blood of Jesus cleanses us from all unrighteousness. Blessed are the pure in heart, for they shall see God. (Matthew 5:8) And the prayer of the righteous person avails or accomplishes much.

Purity in speaking and living God's word kills Satan's plans in our lives and causes Satan to flee from us.

An honest desire for intimacy with God, listening to God, and communicating with God; along with wanting to know what God wants/says, is purity.

Psalm 119:9 reads, how can a young person stay on the path of purity? By living according to God's word.

Do everything without grumbling or arguing, so that you may become blameless and pure, children of God without fault in a warped

and crooked generation. Then you will shine among them like stars in the sky (Phil 2:14-15).

Psalm 24:3 reads: Who may ascend the mountain of the Lord? Who may stand in his holy place? The one who has clean hands and a pure heart, who does not trust in an idol (i.e. money) or swear by a false god.

The fear of the Lord is pure, enduring forever. The decrees of the LORD are firm and all of them are righteous. (Psalm 19:9)

Matthew 22:37-38 Jesus replied, **"Love the Lord your God with all your heart and with all your soul and with all your mind. This is the first and greatest command."**

3. **Perseverance makes prayer powerful.**

Perseverance – Webster's dictionary defines perseverance as persistence (not giving up) in doing something despite difficulty or delay in achieving success.

Continuance of faith in God's word and God's will helps us to see/experience God's victory in our lives. And resisting Satan, causes Satan to flee.

Jesus told us to remain in him and keep his words in us, so we can ask whatever we desire, and it will be done for us. (John 15:7)

And He also said that if we love him, we are to keep His commands (John 14:15).

In Galatians 6:9, we are instructed to not become weary in doing good, for at the proper time we will reap a harvest if we do not give up.

James 1:12 reads, blessed is the one who perseveres under trial, because having stood the test, that person will receive the crown of life that the Lord has promised to those who love him.

In Romans 12:12, we are encouraged to be joyful, patient in affliction, and faithful in prayer.

When we trust in the Lord with all our hearts and lean not on our understanding, in all our ways submitting to God, God will make our paths straight (Proverbs 3:5-6).

In Colossians 1:11, we are encouraged that God wants us to be strengthened with all power, according to his glorious might, so

that we may have great endurance and patience. And we are to stand firm, so we will win life (Luke 21:19).

4. **Praying in the Spirit makes prayer more powerful**. The Holy Spirit intercedes (prays for us) - when we don't know how to pray.

   The bible refers to praying in tongues or praying in the spirit, in 1Corinthians 14:15. As it says, I will pray with my spirit and I will pray with my mind, I will sing with the spirit and I will sing with my mind also. Praying and singing in the spirit taps into more power and makes our prayers more effective, as Satan and ourselves cannot interfere with this heavenly language.

   When new testament believers were baptized with the Holy Spirit they began to speak in tongues. (Acts 2 and Acts 10).

   Luke 11:9-13 reads: **If you then, being evil, know how to give good gifts to your children, how much more will your heavenly Father gives the Holy Spirit to those who ask him?**

As we ask God for his Holy Spirit to live inside of us, we are gifted with the Holy Spirit and receive guidance from the Spirit for praying.

Praying in tongues is a way to pray in which our spirit cries out to God, in a language only God fully understands (and Satan does not understand at all). It also helps us to praise God perfectly.

5. **Praying and fasting make prayer more powerful.**

Fasting - doing without food (or certain foods) as a tribute to God, can take us into a closer relationship with God. Fasting shows we are serious about what it is we are praying for. It draws us into a deeper relationship with God and may help Us and God to listen more closely.

Ezra 8:23 of the Holy Bible reads: So, we fasted and sought our God concerning this matter, and He listened to our entreaty (humble request).

Therefore, fasting with prayer can help in making a way through a barrier.

In Matthew 6, of the Bible, Jesus said, **"When you fast, anoint** (put oil on) **your head and wash your face so that your fasting will not be noticed by men, but by your Father who is in heaven; and your Father who sees what is done in secret will reward you."**

6. **Praying in Pairs of Two, or More** - with other Believers in Jesus Christ **makes for powerful prayer.**

   Praying with other believers in Christ Jesus, builds our faith and encourages us. For in Hebrews 11:6, it reads: Without faith, it is impossible to please God and he who comes to God must believe that God is and that God is a rewarder of those who seek him.

   Jesus himself said, as noted in Matthew 18:19-20 of the Holy Bible, **"Again I say unto you, that if two of you shall agree on earth as touching anything that they shall ask, it shall be done for them by my Father, which is in heaven. For where two or three are gathered, in my name, there I am - in the middle of them."**

Praying in the name of Jesus Christ gives power to prayer.

This is the most significant aspect of effective/powerful praying.

God hears us, because of our **belief in God's son Jesus Christ, God's word, and what Jesus did for Us.*

Satan was defeated and we were forgiven at Jesus' death and resurrection. Satan must obey when we use the authority God gave us and use the name of Jesus Christ because Satan was defeated at the cross.

There is power in the name of Jesus Christ or Christ Jesus.

Jesus said, **"In my name, they shall cast out devils."** (Mark 16:17) He also said in Luke 10:20, **"Do not rejoice because evil spirits obey you; instead rejoice because your names are written in heaven."** Jesus further said, (in John 14:14) **"Whatsoever ye shall ask in my name, I will do it."**

Jesus also said of the future time, (meaning after the death & resurrection of Jesus) **"And in that day ye** (you) **will ask me nothing.**

Verily, (meaning most assuredly or truly), **I say to ye, whatsoever you ask the Father,** (meaning God) **in my name** (meaning Jesus Christ) **He** (meaning God) **will give you.**

Part 5 – Model Prayer (the Lord's Prayer)

In Mathew 6:9-13 and Luke 11:2-4, the bible tells us Jesus said to pray like this:

Our Father in heaven, hallowed be thy name. May thy kingdom come, and thy will be done on earth as it is in heaven. Give us this day, our daily bread. Forgive us our sins, as we forgive those who sin against us. Lead us not into temptation. Instead, deliver us from evil.

Praying this way, we do the following:

1. We give God the recognition as a holy/all-powerful, loving, and magnificent King, to be revered and respected.
2. We ask for God's rule and authority and God's will to be accomplished on earth as it is accomplished in heaven.
3. We ask God to provide His word, food, and finances (anything we need) each day.
4. We ask God to forgive our sins, while we do our best (with God's help) to forgive those who sin against us.
5. We ask God to keep us from being tempted and to protect us from evil.

In summary, God is for Us! According to Genesis 1:26-28 of the Holy Bible, we are created in God's image and God's likeness - male and female. And God wants a relationship with Us.

Prayer is our means of connecting with God, who is three in one: our Creator, our Savior (Christ Jesus), and our Comforter (the Holy Spirit).

There are many types of prayer/ways to communicate with God, such as praise, thanksgiving, petition, intercession, confession, agreement, acknowledgment, tongues, and authority.

Things like sin, distractions, and Satan, can interfere with our prayers and our relationship with God.

Certain behaviors of our own can improve our prayer effectiveness and our relationship with God, such as: making God a priority, living and speaking in ways that please God, confessing sin, forgiving, being thankful, resisting Satan, asking God to keep us from temptation/evil, putting on the full armor of God, honoring the sabbath, and praying with gusto.

Seven power points of prayer are praise, purity, perseverance, praying in the Spirit, fasting, praying in pairs, and praying in the name of Jesus.

As we recognize God's loving, capable, magnificent kingship, and God's power, (while inviting God to accomplish His will in our lives), we can rest and be assured of His loving care.

Blessings to you as you develop a deeper relationship with God!

Bonnie

Resources:

Easton's Bible Dictionary (1), The Holy Bible, various translations, Webster's Dictionary, Strong's Concordance, Google Search Engine, Bible Hub.Com